NIRANJANA DEVI

The Voice of a Soaring Soul

First Published in June 2023

ISBN: 978-93-5741-233-9

BLUEROSE PUBLISHERS
www.BlueRoseONE.com
info@bluerosepublishers.com
+91 8882 898 898

Cover Design:
Aman Sharma

Typographic Design:
Namrata Saini

Distributed by: BlueRose, Amazon, Flipkart

Poet's Note

From the curious child, I used to see in the mirror, I have come far today.

This work took its time to emerge from within me. History and Literature showed gazillion ways to define and interpret poetry. However, the simple common key to good poetry is, I believe, empathy - the more I try to see what is in you, the more you understand my words.

I admit great writers have inspired some verses in this book. I couldn't turn my back on the eerie mystery in the gravediggers of Shakespeare, and the nostalgia in Kamala Das's grandmother's house. I can only hope that my audience would feel it too.

My Guruji taught me that the entire universe lies within each of us, so we are all interconnected. But somewhere along the way, those connectors dried up and hence the world is now in chaos. My prayer is that my poems, along with other good-hearted words and deeds, water them so that the world may once again stand united.

So, I offer my voice through my words, to those who think they are now voiceless.

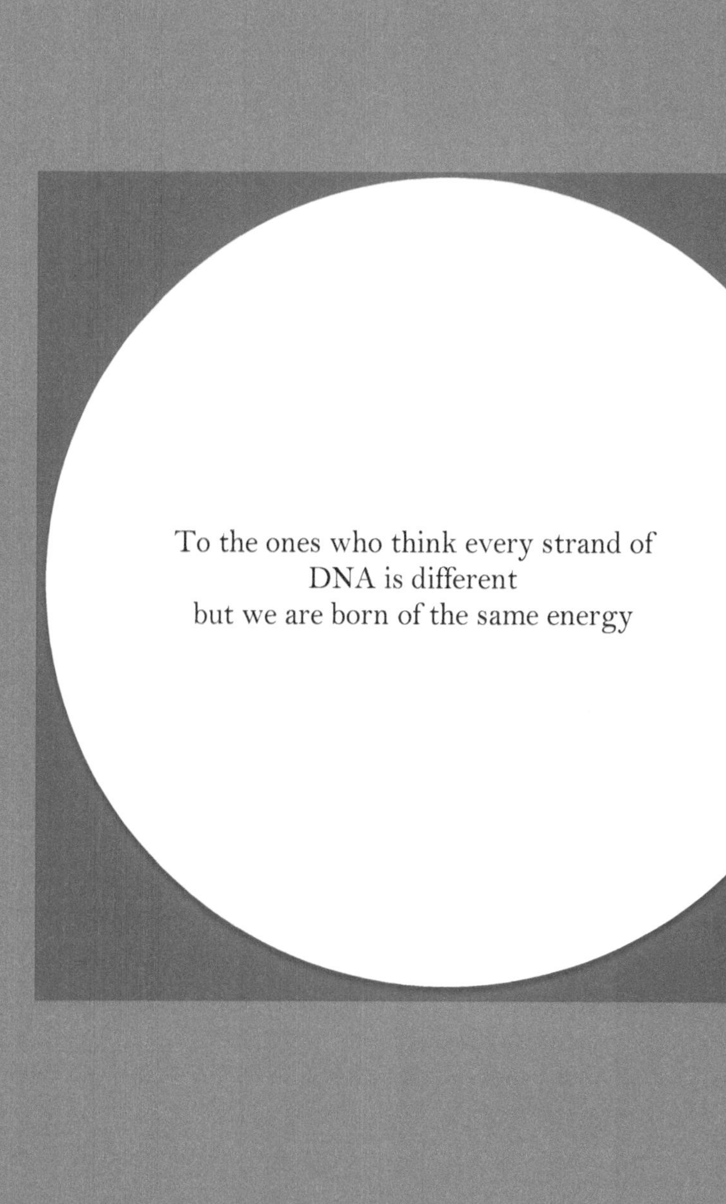
To the ones who think every strand of
DNA is different
but we are born of the same energy

Contents

Cobwebs

Burning as it is
The early sun shines
Radiant and ready to soar.

Walking along the hedges
Squinting my eyes
I could hear the owls snore.

To the tree-house, the tree-house
Fruit of our childhood days
I reminisced in its smell.

The rope ladder with knots
Now looks withered
Untouched for years.

Up the Wooden Castle,
I felt home than ever
Tasting the dust as I roamed.

The roof looks hoary
Like my soul- perplexed
In a mesh of cobwebs.

These wooden planks have stories
Memories- happy and sad
Secured by the cobwebs.

When the rain pours,
The water trickles from the roof
To the silver lines of the webs.

The inside of the roof
Turns into a pearl chandelier, which breaks
And fills the floor when it gets heavy.

The mesh in my soul
I see in the cobwebs- connected
As the green to the Spring Spirit.

Opportunities, Obstacles
The lines of my webs
Complete my puzzle called Life.

Chaos or Choices
I feel secure inside
That labyrinthine guide.

Cobwebs of twenty years
Have given me addictions
That I cannot wish away.

Cobwebs of twenty years
My home- still in making
The mess that makes me feel beautiful.

So long so pure has it been
In me, in our tree-house
Stuck to every inch of me.

I see them in nature too
Amidst the dense green leaves-
Everything, everyone lives among cobwebs.

Gloom, glee, plight, pleasure
I wish my coffin be
As messy as my soul.

Just A Mile Ahead

Just a mile ahead
The dawn is not that far
Fate has been wicked
Near is the end, of the war.

Dark to hoary to light
Eager mouths to devour
We haven't failed us
So do not be vexed.

Leaves may shed, trees may fall
All for better, not worse
Pull yourself out of the past
Cast yourself out of the shadows.

The storm is stronger than ever
All the senses, blinded
Win these walls over
Align your conscience.

Roads paved with flesh and blood
Corrupted souls burden the earth
Unaware of the joy and calm

They crawl, as ignorant toads.

Villains disguised as heroes
Peacekeepers stumbling so low
Concerns may not be true
Numerous bodies to tow away.

Move your legs forward
Help those who lost it
Show mercy before they beg
Their smiles will be your best reward.

Sky will soon be clear
Of all the noise and smoke
Rivalry brings only tears
Let your soul have your voice.

Come, strive for the horizon
There will be your bed of solace
Rise and defend your kindred
It's just a mile ahead.

What's Beyond Be Gay

Hark! That noise of the pedantic vultures
Look up and see the everlasting sky
White is now red- not just in the borders
It then turns black along with the pained cry.

Down you stare and see dust, dry of moisture
There once might have been a gleaming river
Barks of once-trees near have lost their texture
Fauna must have fled by lurking terror.

Terror? Asks he, who craves for more every time
Disastrous 'he' calls himself Conqueror
Keeps building to describe what is sublime
Fails to know, for Poor, pain's not yet pleasure.

Man tends to live in the periphery
Desires to defeat the pacing steed-Time
Searches for the holy grail of Mary
Realizes not what his soul inside, chimes.

To see, to know, to hear, to feel beyond
You, O destroyer, look into yourself
You've been missing what you are to expound
'Tis harder than dusting your old bookshelf.

You are, but for all, a waiting Mortal
For that short anticipated moment
The hour maybe dark but make it royal
The sticks and stones will be there to torment.

And yet if you live for the obvious cause
To heal Mother Earth of all ill and gloom
We don't need any necessary pause
To see, to know, to hear, to feel the bloom.

There will be no more cries out in the sky
Clarity will wash over us, and then
The day's come when no tongues need to be tied
Every man can breathe warmly in his den.

Bury me as I die by that river
That bank where the cicadas still might cry
And the trees by the breeze still might quiver
What's beyond be gay; hope with which I'd lie.

The Fire

Do you see the smoke rising
Over those hills in distance
Do you know why it's red?
It is not just our eyes.

There's yet more ground to cover
To find our brothers and sisters
Fear nothing that comes at you
Our destiny is near.

Let the lightning be your torch
Let the storm be your guide
This is our fight to survive
Against the odds.

Let your fear out as warcries
Let your doubts turn to ash
This is our moment to get back
What we lost long ago.
Our fathers built the roof above us
Our mothers made their homes for us
The Nature taught us to exist
And then we rose against Her.

That smoke is from her Fire
Her wrath is that of a Mother
Cleansing her spawns of ill,
Decayed and dead inside.

The children had it coming
Deserving every burn and sizzle
But realize- the sparks from the Fire
Will remake every bone in them.

A Child

I see a child.
I see the child sitting, light as air,
Under the leaf, the roof of that treehouse.
I see the child counting little grains
Of sand, meditating on the work.
I see the child looking at the sky
Waiting to change its colour.
I see the child glancing across the plain
For a tired mother returning from work.

I see the child smiling and guessing
What sweet mother will bring today.
I see the child looking down
At the broken ladder.
I see the child wondering
How to get down.
I see the child stuck
In between the earth and the sky.
I see the child almost in tears out of fear.
I see the child remembering the steps.
I see the child remembering the roots.
I see the child gaining trust in self.

I see the child stepping down with determination.

I see the child running towards the mother's voice.

I see the child hugging her as if she was the only lifeline.

I see the child.

I see me.

Live It Till Your Last Breath

The hour has gone dark my brother
To even hope for a ray of light
To feel the sun on the bare skin
Oh, it's a plight.

Look around, look at the soldiers
Lying cold on the red ground
But their shrieking voices
Oh, hear that ringing sound.

It is time for us to choose
Whether to give in or give up
Or to fight back for what's ours
With whatever we have left in us.

The darkness may be frightening
But brother, the dawn's not far
You were born for this very reason.

Live it till your last breath
There's nowhere to run and hide
So live it till your last breath.

The noise is deafening, my brother
The bashes, the roars and the cries
Of hope, of victory, and of pain.

The blood they spilled so fearlessly
For our lives, for this world
Stories of legends, our brothers
They inspire us for the fights of the future

The world is ours and now
It's our turn to protect it
For our children to live well
May all the chaos fall behind them.

A Maiden

The rays caressed her from the West
Birds were flying back to their nest
She stared at them; those red hairs
Falling over her face in layers.

She stared at them for long
Listened closely to their song
What could they have to sing about?
Most of them however end up shot.

They fly, soaring aimless
Blessed to be so tameless
Here she stands on the soft sand
Bare and free: she can but pretend.

What's that on her ankles- shackles?
On her wrists too- they cackle-
As they move about, hurting her
Adorned in her blood, a crimson blur.

Tamed to be timid, never tough
Reminded by the heavy metal cuffs
She is not allowed to hope
Not to even dream to elope.

Her smiles stole long back
Other noises, loud in her shack
Her laugh icy and forced
Until she forgets remorse.

Her hair could feel the humid air
Dancing like fire; too ignorant to care
She looked up to the moon
A maiden waiting for a boon.

Out Out Brief Candle!

Out Out Brief Candle!
The sad Bard whined
Don't be offended
Brevity suits you.

Comrade of Death
Invincible in spirit
Don't be fooled
You have no one else.

Spend the mortal days
Making history immortal
Don't sit still
Leave that to Emotion.

Lord Gravedigger

The black coats mourn and sniff
reminiscing about the dead's life
While he digs the perfect hole
In the land of green and stone.

What's so much to brag about?
He wonders as he works his art
Little is one in the pool of lives
Little is one in the pool of dead.

The blacklings kiss and offer the body
Coffin to live and flowers to breathe
How long do they think it will last,
He hides his smile as he shifts the soil.

Visitors leave the holy ground soon
As soon as he begins to cover it,
Welcoming the newbie to the world
Ruled by Lord Gravedigger.

"My crumbled loved ones", he addresses
As the night blankets the land,
Let's begin our celebrations
To make our fresh comrade at home.

You must have stories to tell,
He urges the soulless fickle being,
Who stays below the bed of mud
Having no clue of what now.

Fear not, run not, scream not, child
For I am your Lord Protector
A gravedigger by day and night
But a humble keeper of nature's waste.

You need not feel so confused
This world is simpler than the past
No pain, nor ecstasy or blood
Only Silence and its Solace.

Here you dream for hours and days
Of your little daughter's marriage
Of your companion's stronger life
Never knowing the complexities of it.

Here you make friends very soon
A thief, a reformer, a king, in the past
All converse in the same dead whispers
With no difference in their accents.

They share with me sometimes
As would you, soon I hope, about
The treacherous place they hail from
And the peace I provide them here.

What of you that still have life
Is sucked deep into the plethora
Where it will be assigned again
To go through all the mundane of life.

Did you forget to leave your mark?
It will be for better, I tell you
For if you do, then you will keep dying
Over and over, wrung out by thick heads.

Had you lived humble and strived
For the truth to be accepted by all
Then you never have a thing
In your cold life, as chaos.

All In. All One.

A bit extreme I felt,
When i saw him cursing himself
For loving his God so much
That he lost everything to it.

Did he lose? What did he lose?
Money? Name? Status?
If so, then he is doomed
To think of them as a loss.
Good riddance it is, you see.

God made you
Without spending Money
Without using Name
Without exploiting Status
Because God has none of these.

It is Man, his most pampered creation
Who measures life's value
With things made of substance,
Least bothered about virtue
That he can taste
Only with his heart and soul.

So where exactly are we?
Heaven, where we are happy
For being kind?
Or Hell, where we are miserable
For our vices?
Do we need to learn to fly, to dive
To reach these places?

It is all inside us, no doubt.
The darkness of Hell and
The Light of Heaven.
Who we choose to be leads us
To one or the other.
But to live in the moment,
You need to feel the Earth.

Being one with Nature
Learn the rhythm
Of the Heart of Living
That beats in all of us,
The voice of the Primal Energy
Urging us to be present and alive.

A Mere Reflection

Satan, they called you.
You smiled, Knower of Truth
Who are you? Why do you smile?

Is it because you know all,
The deepest and darkest which enthral
The human- mighty and meek-
Who ignores the instinct to seek?

What is that? Remorse?
Hearing the plight, wow so coarse
Of their soared throats and parched tongues
Possessing nothing but heavy lungs
Blaming God and whatnot for their state
Walking towards the Hell's Gate.
Hell's Gate! You laugh about
So cruel it is, that pout
Mocking these tired souls
Who dream of slimy trolls.

Or is that pity-

Knowing you are a mere reflection,

Of humanity's lost affection,

Of the self-caused pains,

O the perishing gains,

Of the self-composed dirge,

Of the impending Merge?

Pitch Black

I close my eyes and I see everything.
Everything is sweet, serene, and sublime.

The sun blinks with his cloud-lids
Turns what it touches into gold
Not too hot and never cold.

The earth so loving
Dense green flows all over
Flowers and vines hover.

The people so happy
Minding their own business
Helping those in distress.

The food so healthy
The breakfast tastes precious
Veggies no longer vicious.
The world so peaceful
Families are together
Children growing better.

I open my eyes I see pitch black.

So dark a world as never,

That I wish to close my eyes forever.

Sprout In Me

Across the river those green beds
Spring blossom showered on them
Patches of grass with pretty decor
And I see them brown and rot.

The blades so dry in the sun
That I could see their veins
The flowers so grey and darker
Than the burnt paper ash.

The sky showed an exact
Of Heaven: Mighty Blue Nest.
Safe as a mother's womb
But I see no colour.

So Dark that I can't know
If it is black or blindness
Surprised that I enjoy it
The dull feel and dread noises.
Conflict- in ad out
Catastrophe- visible or not
Caught up in a dark whim
Called out to the Saviour.

Weeds, oh weeds everywhere
Draining the life out of me
Some part still manages to survive
Sees the green beds and blue roof.

But for how long? Tear me thus, You,
That the stitch between me and Dark
Be destroyed for good
And pull me hard out of whims.

Let the green sprout in me
Instead of the fatal weeds
Let the flowers bloom in me
And serve you wide around.

That Window In The Attic

That window in the attic of my childhood home
Seems all fuzzy in moss above the domed roof
That window in the attic, my looking glass
How then I observed the world beyond.

I woke up in infancy, to gaze up, tiptoeing
And outside I saw butterflies with polka dots
Oh! To fly like them, fluttering along with the breeze
Long green snakes visited at times, but
They couldn't keep me away from there
Not even the shadow of my fading mother.

Time changes all, they say with sadistic sighs
I could never leave it, my happy place!
Until the day I stepped out of that home;
I looked back at it for one last time
Wondering if the infant will look at me
Behind that window, still on her toes.

I return today and I recognize it- not vaguely.
The moss is dry brown, the glass stained brown
Noone missed me behind my looking glass
Noone ever called out to me from up there
I climbed up the dome and reached it
Ran my fingers along, pressing my memories deep.
Now I see through the window from outside.
Staring into my chamber, I see my prison.
From chains to chains, I took myself
Dreaming about butterflies with polka dots
And long green snakes
They can move, why can't I?

Darkest Night

Under the darkest night
Shine the stars brightest
Under the deepest ocean
Thrive the corals their best
My love, don't feel dim now
For you are to rise to height.

You walked with your head
Drooped of shame and sorrow
You forget to remember
To gaze at Nature ad Providence
To pamper your mind with
The serenity around you.

You reject the possibilities
Of luck to caress you
You choose paths away
From those which need you
Just because you feel unsure
Of how it might turn ill again.
Losers keep waiting for
The Moment, to drive them stronger
You, my heavy-hearted one
Don't wish to even desire

A life of gay pictures, which
Would make them jealous.

You rue the time of your birth
You don't realize her now
Passing slowly; wishes for you
To join her tamed steed
She looks back at you in hope
Arms open to lead you on.

You have sobbed enough
You have hurt enough
The blue moon is not so far
But jump and reach for it
Voice your heart's thoughts
Let conscience rule the rest.

The Light In Me

Dawn appears as dusk
Light has turned dark
Thought it was my eyes
But no, it was my mind.

I once craved colours
Now it's all black.
Wearing white felt
Naked inside out.

Fought my way through
With claws and teeth
Never felt the ease
Of the inner calm.

Fell in deep gutters,
Sometimes called lust
Mistakes: all of them
But, it was a passé
That shadow was still there
Following me since birth.
I ask finally, "Who are you?"
I hear "The light in you".

"The reason for your life,
Which you bled and shredded.
It's time to look forward,
When you still have the chance."

The voice was so powerful
Melting me down,
Strengthening me,
From the inside.

White doesn't scare me now
Black almost vanished
Dark seemed not to interfere
While I enjoyed the light.

I took the chance
To soar forward
Now I lead my life
With the light in me.

The Toll Of The Bell

The toll of the bell echoes
Along with the clanging of swords
The air was all dusty and hard
But nothing compared to the odour
Of intense, salty, 'holy' blood.

To what end are you marching forth
Are you certain or have you lost your way?
Are you certain of your claim
To this mysterious voluminous world
Of abstract being and vague doing?

Look at the mess you have made
With your brainless deeds
Orphans run along the deserted homes
Who will take care of them?
Why do you still hold it tight
The weapon that brought the doom
Your ego, your 'self', your actions
Has your soul turned black too?

Pray for some light to shine
In your body, mind and soul
This world still needs you
Shouldn't we pick the pieces up?

The universe is yet mysterious
You have a lot to absorb yet
Not evil, but the goodness
Aren't you coming along?

Wait For The Time

Sane souls who claim happy
Have they felt it in their sap?
Smiles gleam with sorrows
We live but a clown's life
Juggling for applause.

In the midst of dusty haste,
We see blood-spitting lives
Miserable until the end
Crushed and torn apart
Cleared off from the earth.

In this alleged New Age

Revolution starts from tyranny

For tyranny- Ends in tyranny!

Millions suffer for a few

Millions not even newsworthy.

Lies become plain truth by exertion

Assaults- shredded papers in the bin

Gods and religions, ground for crime as ever

The few keep on hunting the millions

This is our dream world now.

Wait for the time,

Hands and minds will rise,

Be devoid of ignorance,

Purged from the sins of past and present-

We will rise and fly high.

Who But He

There I stand at the edge of a cliff
Thinking about what's past than what's in front
My armour seems at once so rogue and stiff
Million reasons floating around to taunt.

There I stand against the high mighty breeze
Freezing all in me, on me, to the core
Had I lashed back at the tormenting tease
Might I now have stood o a less lofty shore?

Dance to chance, bear to care, kill if I will
Sure lived the life of a tempted maiden
Was I walking in the wrong shoes until?
Should I feel the joy to be cast off Eden?

Truth, but oh, the world's Rights jinxed its Wrongs
Who, but He, to use Morality Tong.

Acknowledgement

IF you have read my verses, you might think I'm not a happy soul.

However, I am three feet off the ground happy that I feel His energy in me - unequivocally grateful to the One True Absolute Guru, Adishunybalashakti. My body, mind and soul together realize that without His energy, I am nothing.

I couldn't have done this without my closest family. My husband, Rahul and his family were kind enough to support all my craziness and I believe him when he says he is happy to be my eternal lifeline. My mothers, Renuka and Rejitha, who truly define 'mother' stood by all the good decisions I made in my life and also gave me space to correct the bad ones myself without judging me. I enjoy the perks of being in a joint family. My grandmother, Leela Bai, has been my idol of how versatile a woman could be. My siblings - Omkaralexmi, Meenakshi, Savitha and Seena- keep me on my toes, so thank you, chipmunks.

I am truly in debt to the support system I receive from my Thapovanam Siddhashramam family. They are the source and keepers of the actual knowledge about the entire Being. I can't thank them enough for their love and service to the world.

This book won't see the world without the assistance of Blue Rose Publishers. Thank you for supporting budding writers like me to bring out their share to the world. You are indeed doing a wonderful thing.

To each individual who hopes, and acts on it, that one day this world will be a paradise with only divine love and nothing else, I thank you in advance. I am forever ready to join you.